AF583737

Because of those who came before me, for those who will follow me. Remember we are our ancestors' wildest dreams.—Marlee

To the curious learners, may we write the next chapters together with kwop koort (good hearts).—Rhys

Scholastic Press
An imprint of Scholastic Australia Pty Limited (ABN 11 000 614 577)
PO Box 579 Gosford NSW 2250
www.scholastic.com.au

Part of the Scholastic Group
Sydney • Auckland • New York • Toronto • London • Mexico City
New Delhi • Hong Kong • Buenos Aires • Puerto Rico

Published by Scholastic Australia in 2024.

ISBN: 978-1-76026-527-4

A catalogue record for this book is available from the National Library of Australia

Typeset in Dustyland and Calliope MVB.
Book design by Sofya Karmazina.

Rhys Paddick created these illustrations digitally.

Scholastic Press acknowledges the Traditional Owners of Country throughout Australia. We pay our respects to Elders past and present, and remember that First Nations peoples are the original storytellers of this land. This always was and always will be Aboriginal land.

Printed in China by RR Donnelley.
Scholastic Australia's policy, in association with RR Donnelley, is to use papers that are renewable and made efficiently from wood grown in responsibly managed forests, so as to minimise its environmental footprint.

10 9 8 7 6 5 4 3 2 1 24 25 26 27 28 / 2

A Scholastic Press book from Scholastic Australia

FOR 60,000 YEARS

Marlee Silva
Rhys Paddick

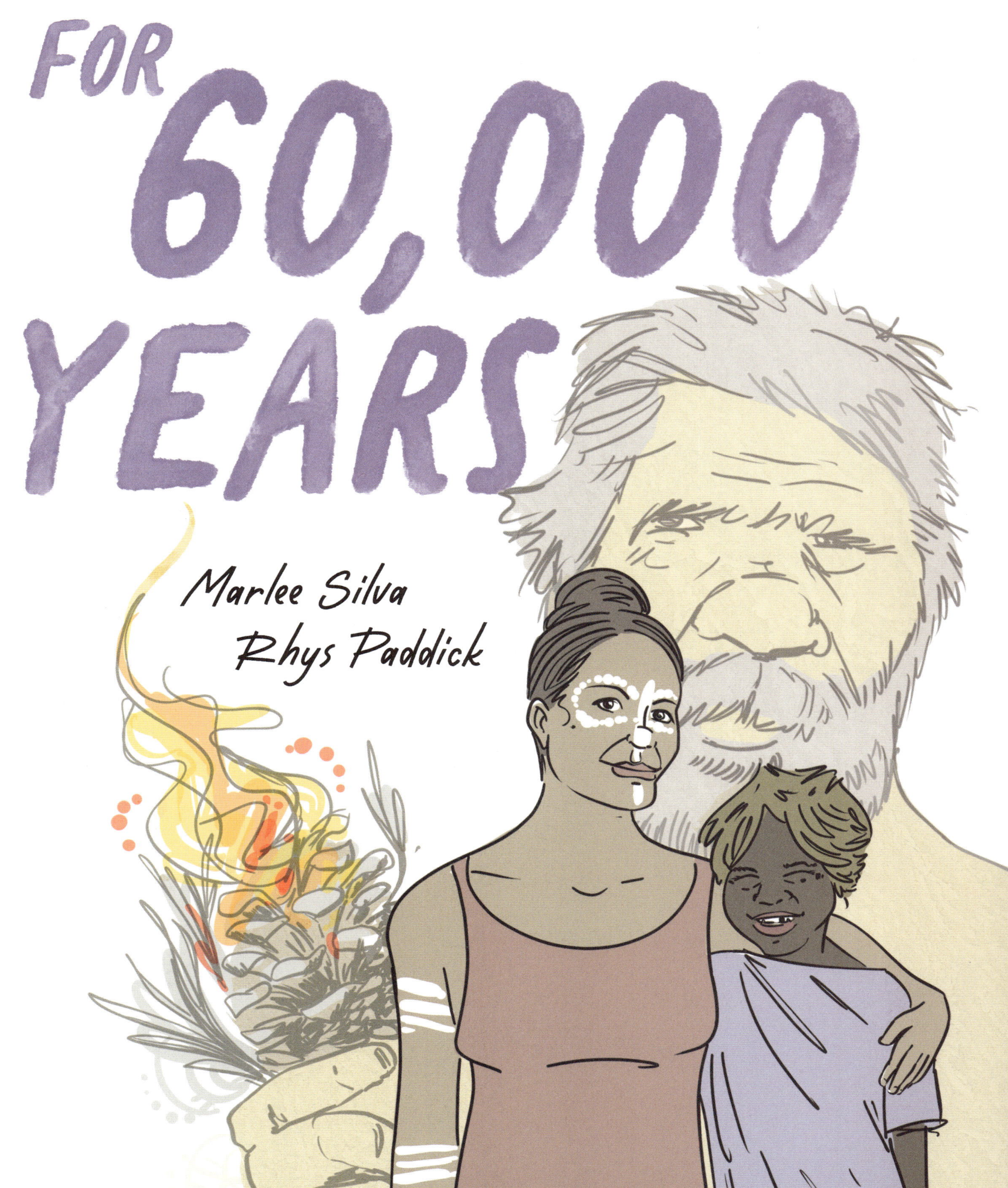

For 60,000

years,

as sure as **the sun**

rises and rests,

my people have thrived,

they have survived,

emerging stronger

than the best.

A couple hundred years ago,
ghosts
sailed in,
called it 'Sydney Cove.'

My people were there
on the shore,
living in **peace**,
no need to wish
for more.

But they saw not us,
only our beautiful land.

To them, she was
a shiny treasure trove.

They moved us off our homes,
made us ill,
counted us with
plants and animals . . .

they took our will.
WILSON.
KING

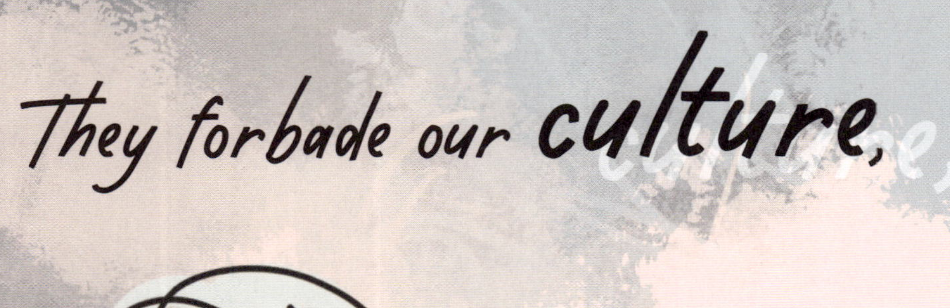

They forbade our **culture**,

tried to break

our souls.

They took our language,
our dance,
our songs . . .

and worst of all,

was our **children**

whom they stole.

In classrooms and boardrooms,

on football fields
and running
tracks,

in government
and galleries,

on stage

and on screen.

My people are **proud** in their success
and in the ways that
they fight back.

Oh, how their **greatness**
must be seen!

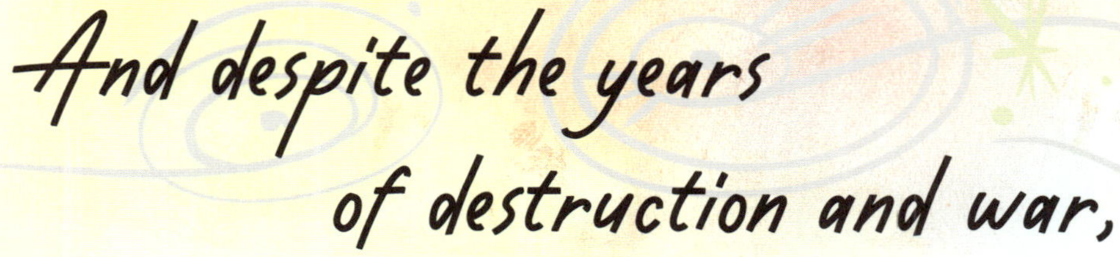

And despite the years
of destruction and war,

despite the horrors
and pain that we bore . . .

As sure as the sun rises and rests,

my people will **thrive** and **survive**. . .

for 60,000 years **more**.